Merry
CHRISTMAS

This Books Belongs To

....

....

....

....

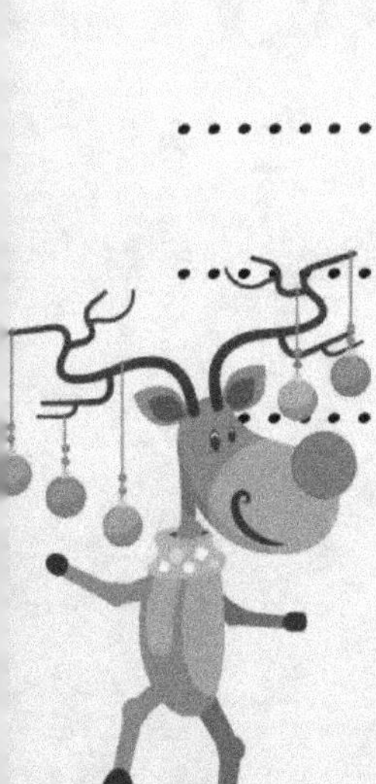

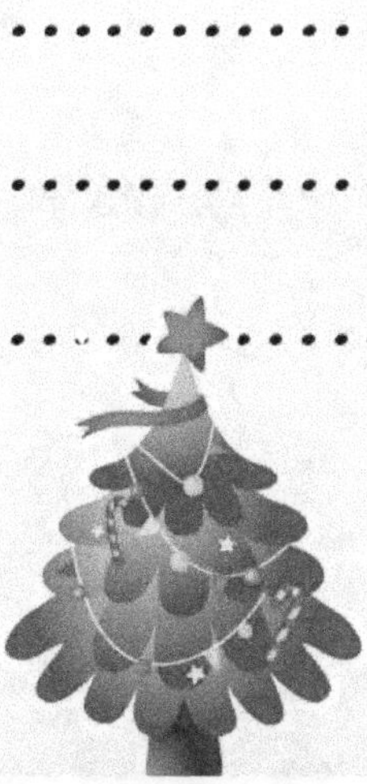

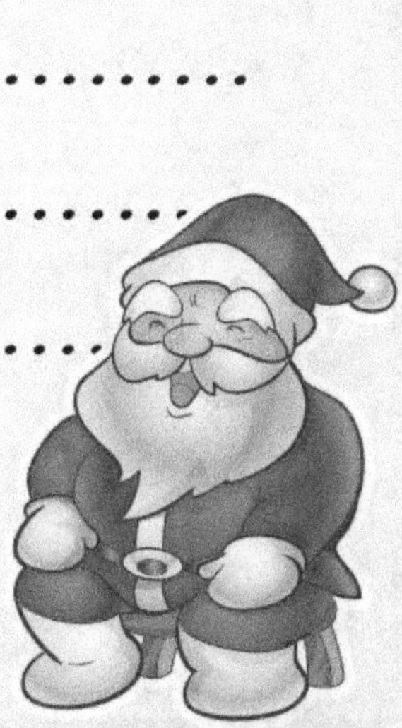

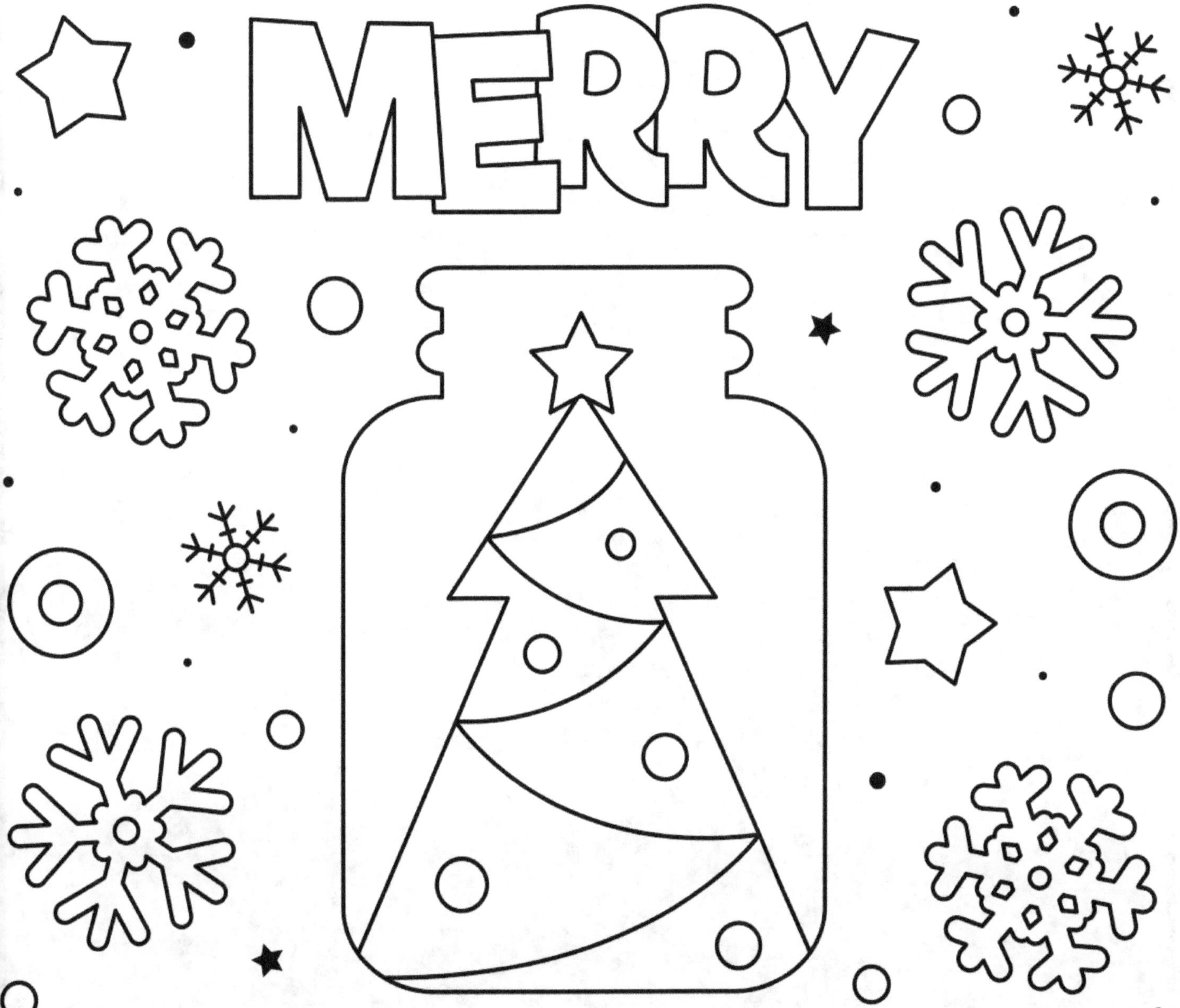
MERRY
CHRISTMAS

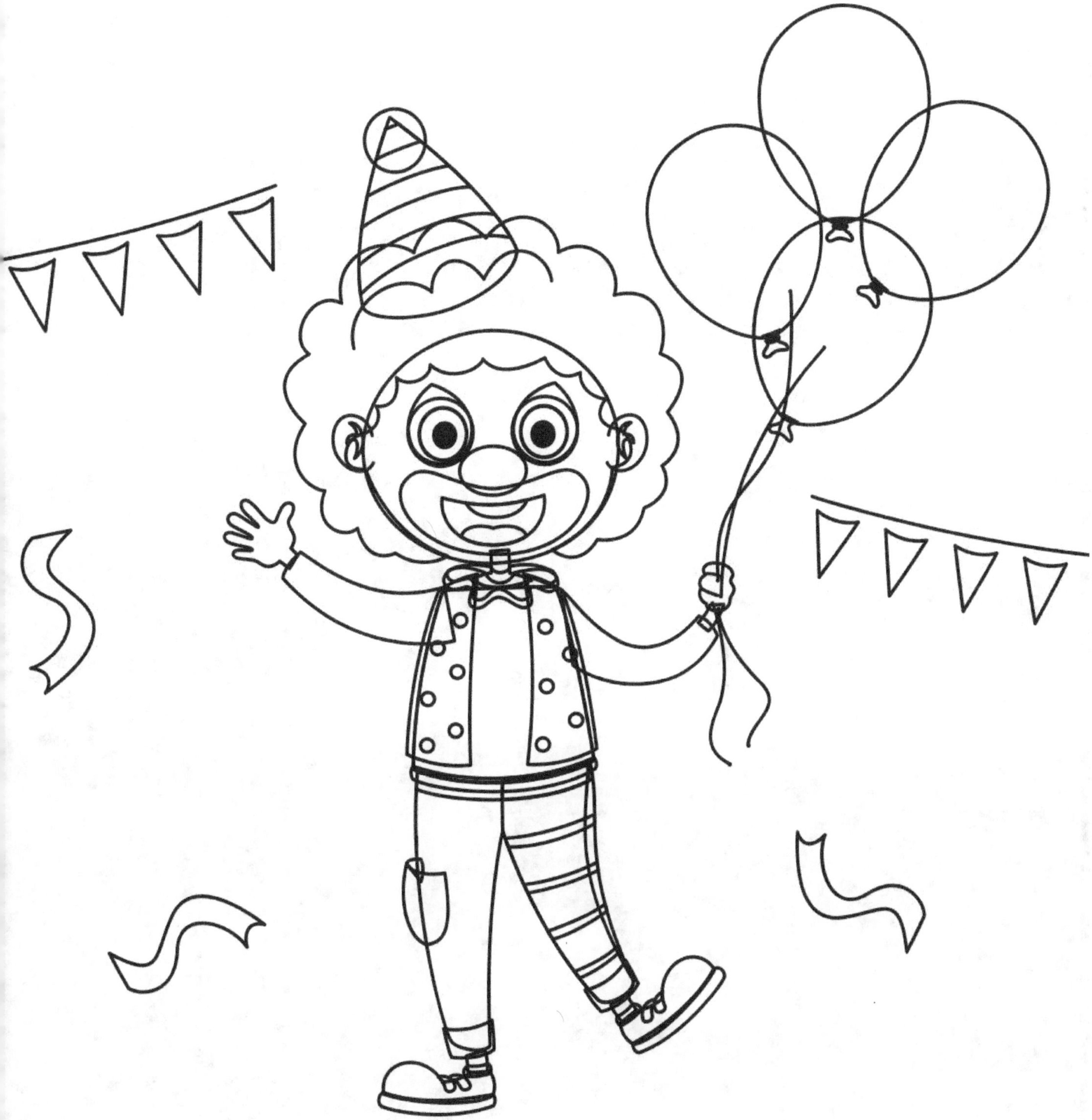

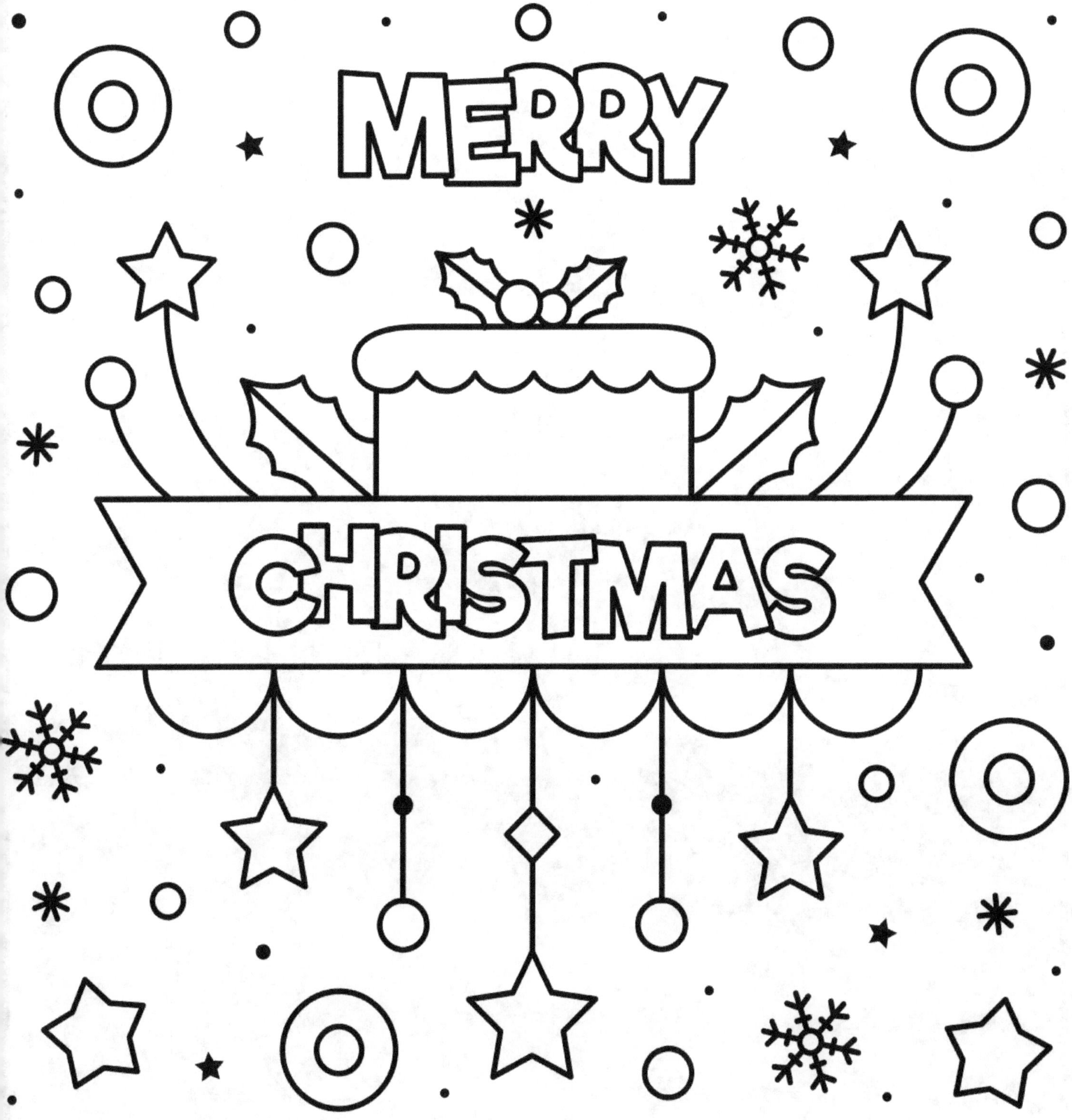
MERRY
CHRISTMAS

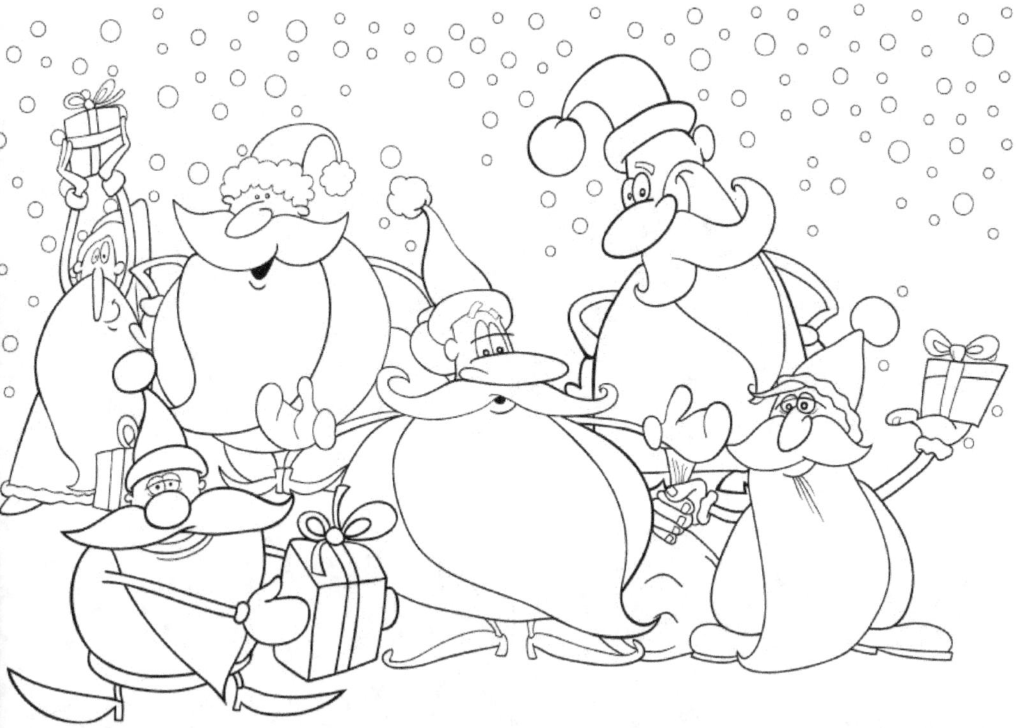

FIND 7 DIFFERENCES

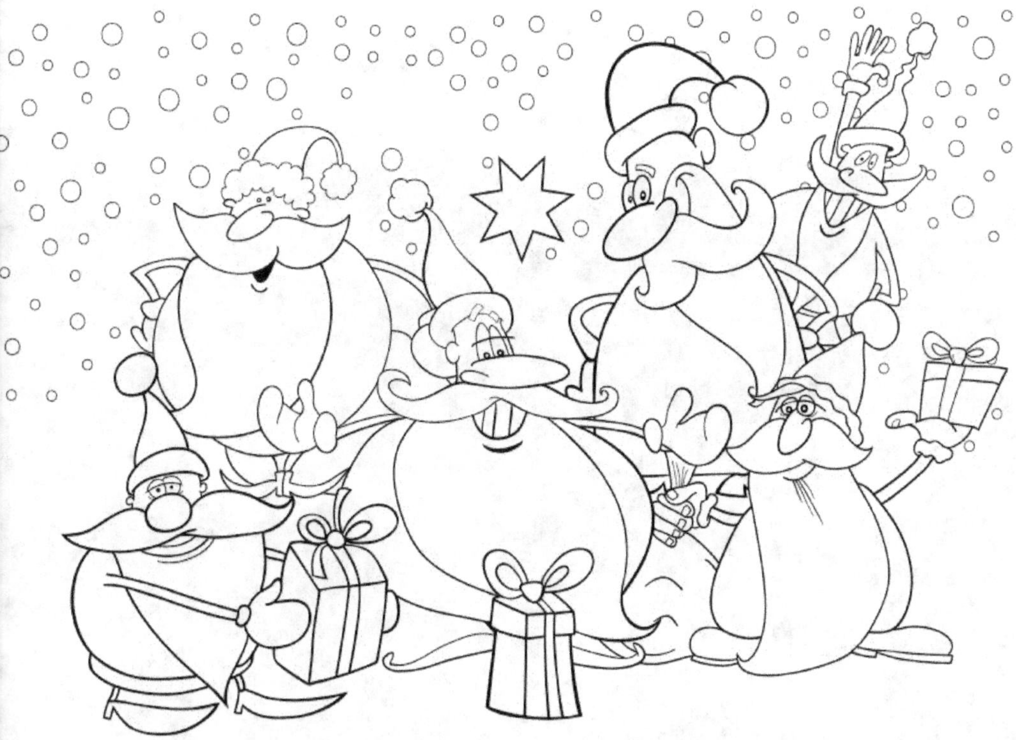

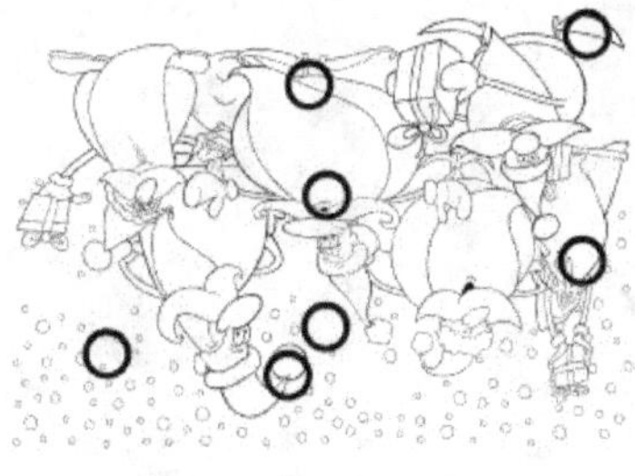

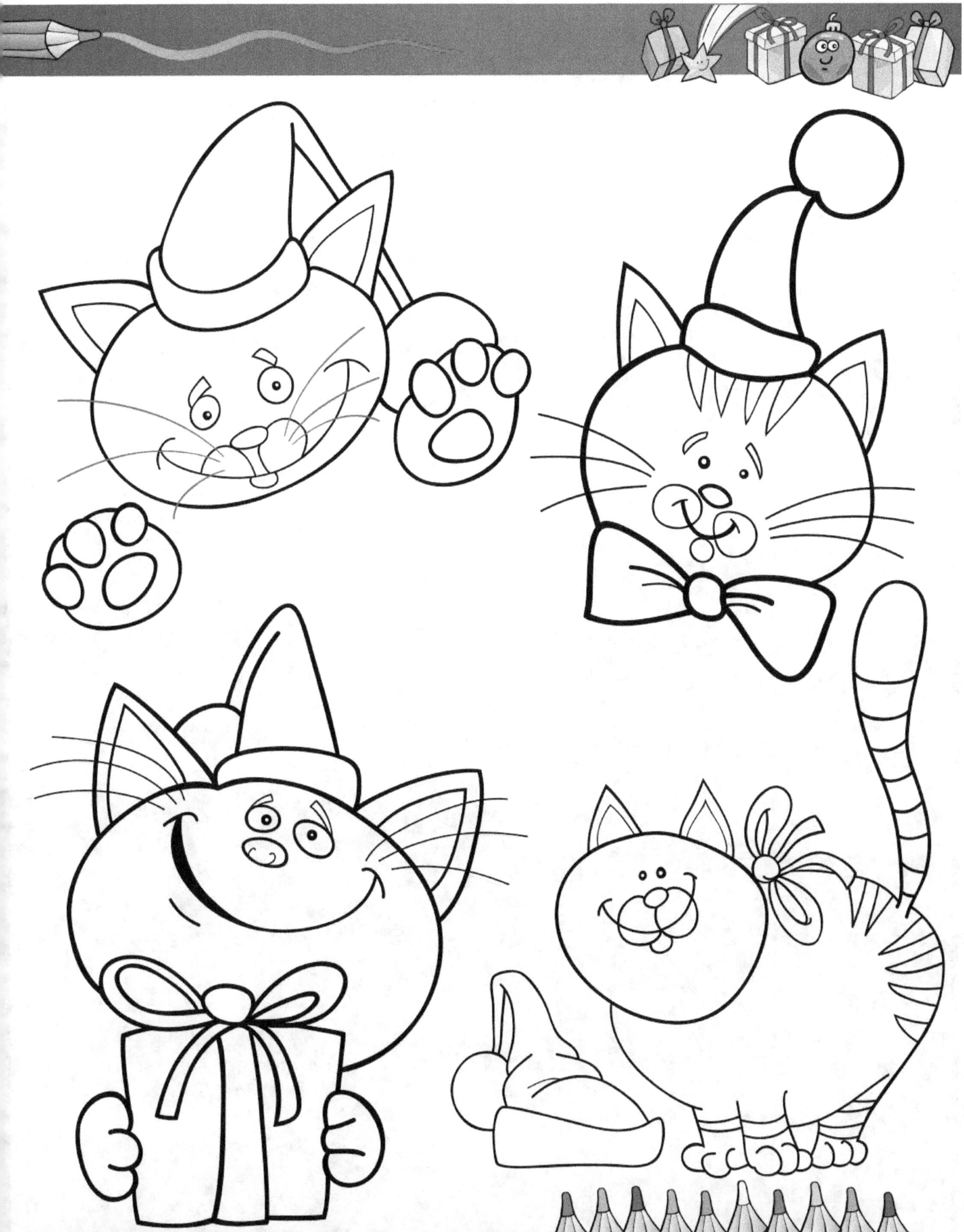

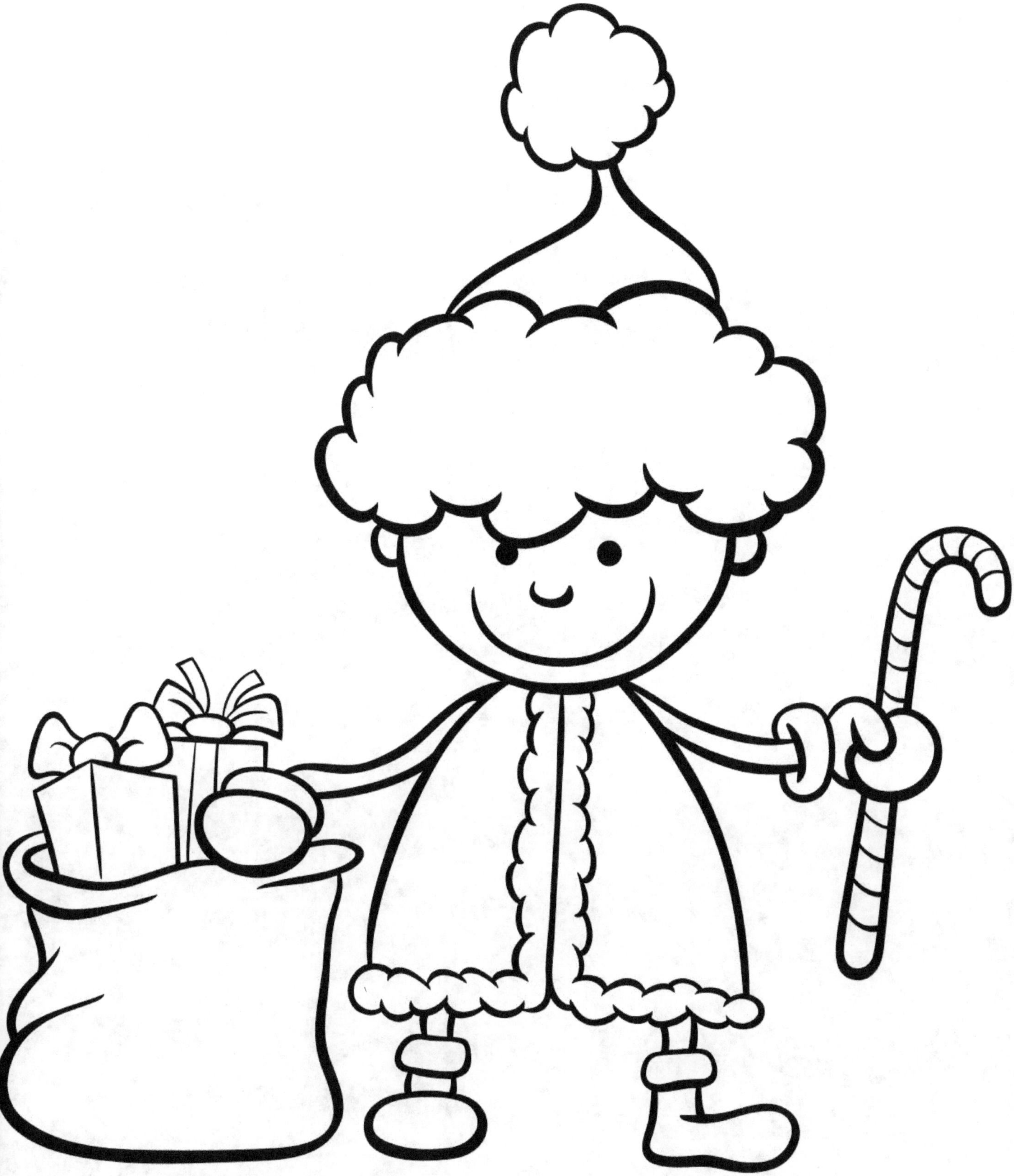

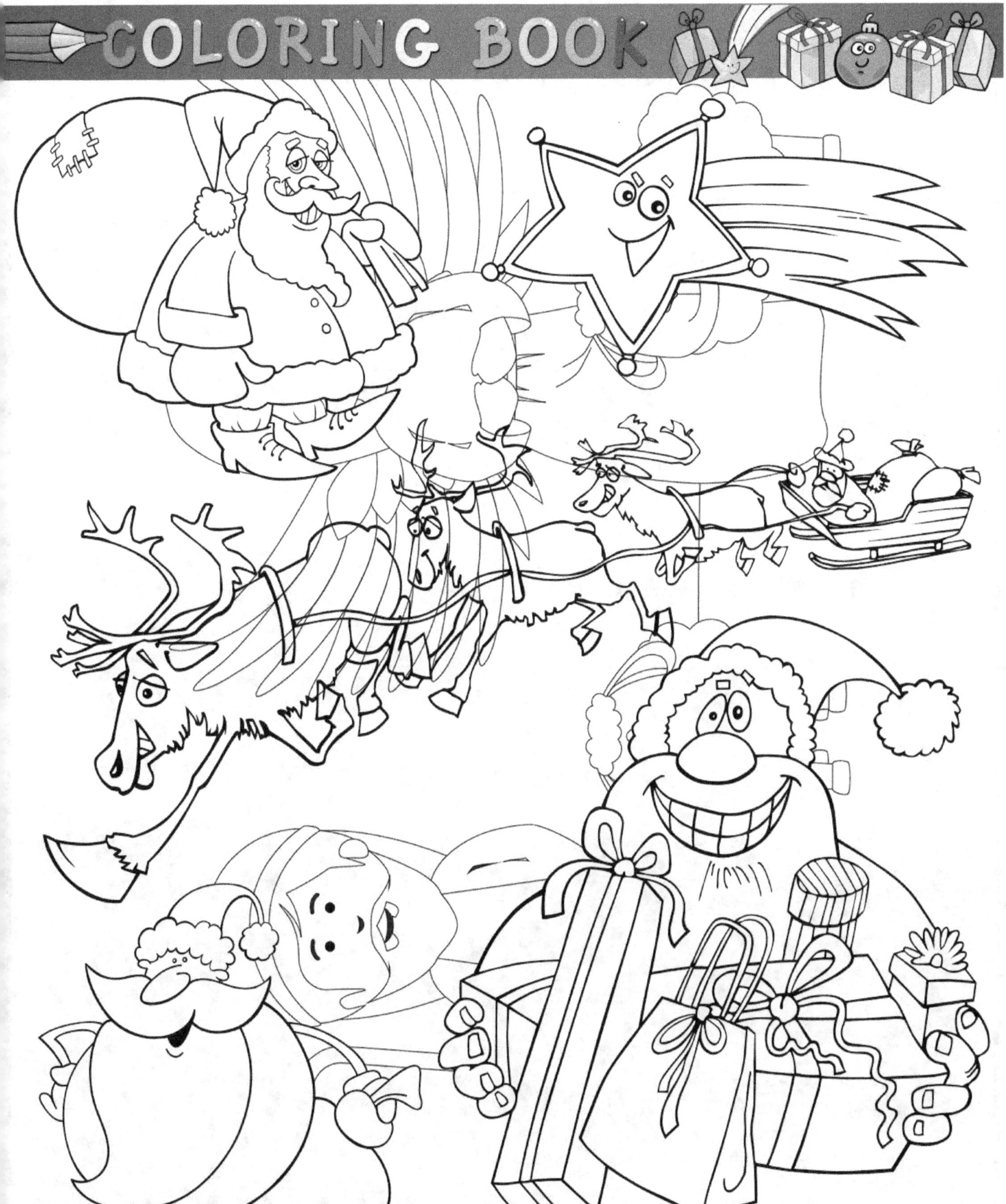

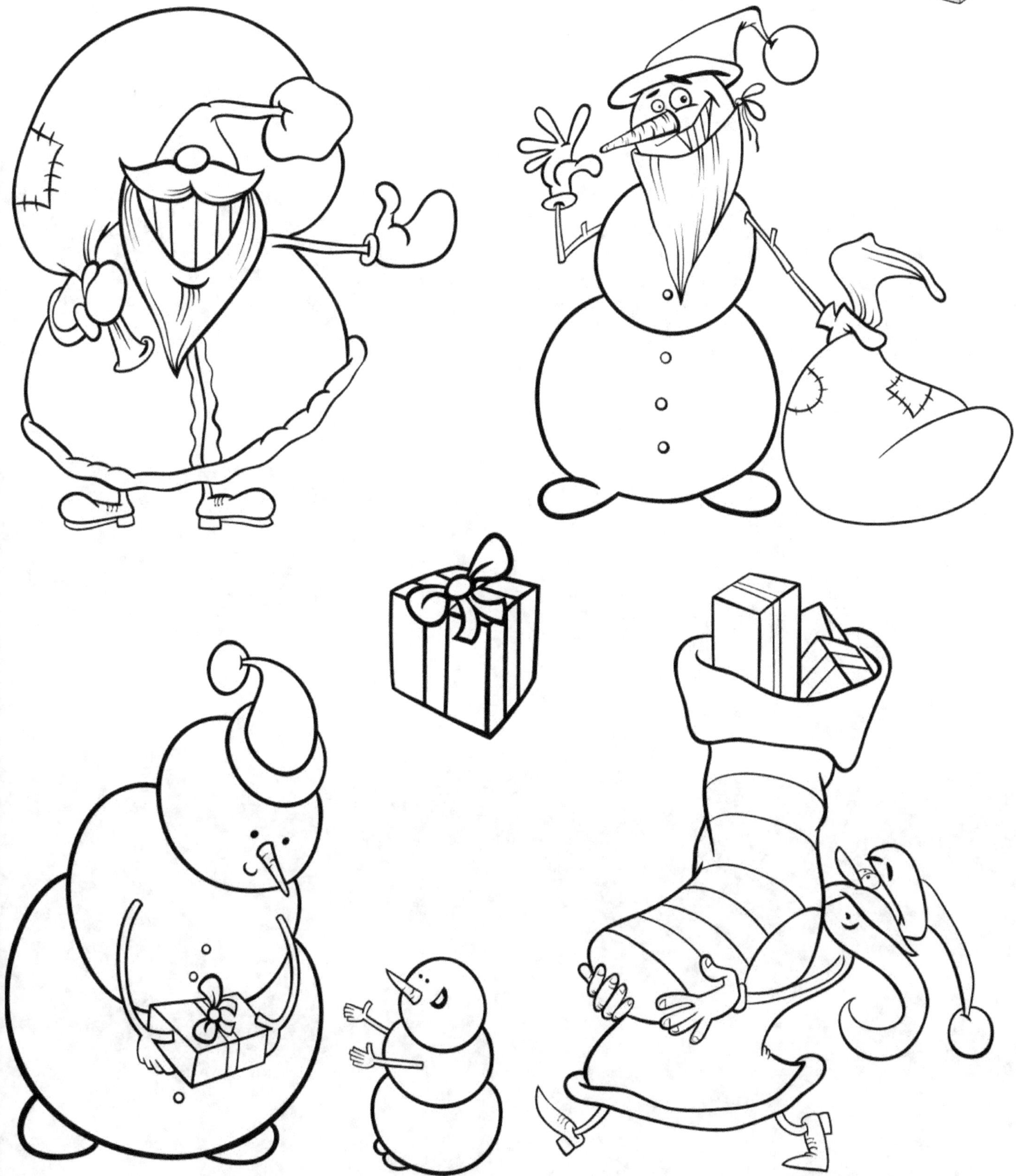

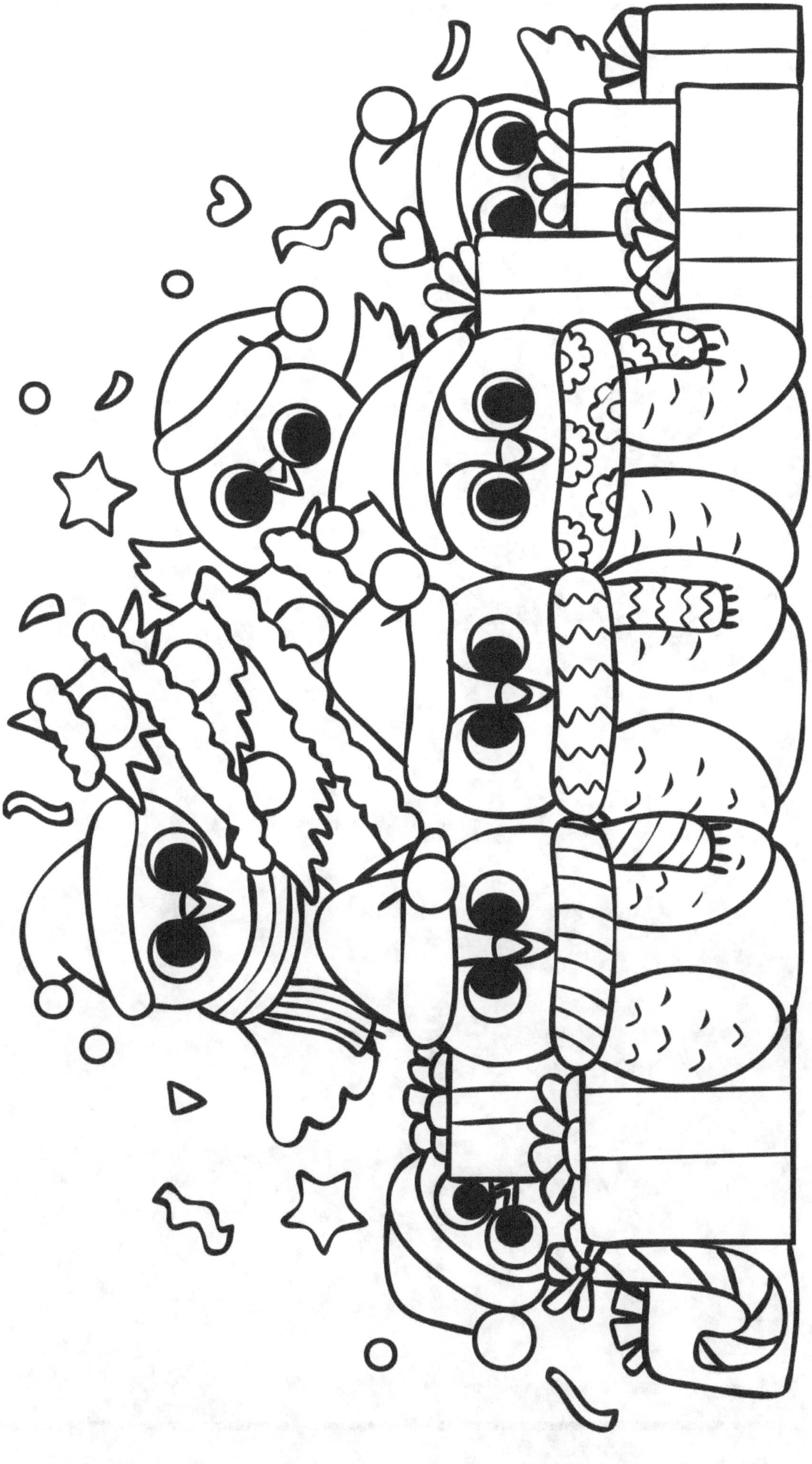

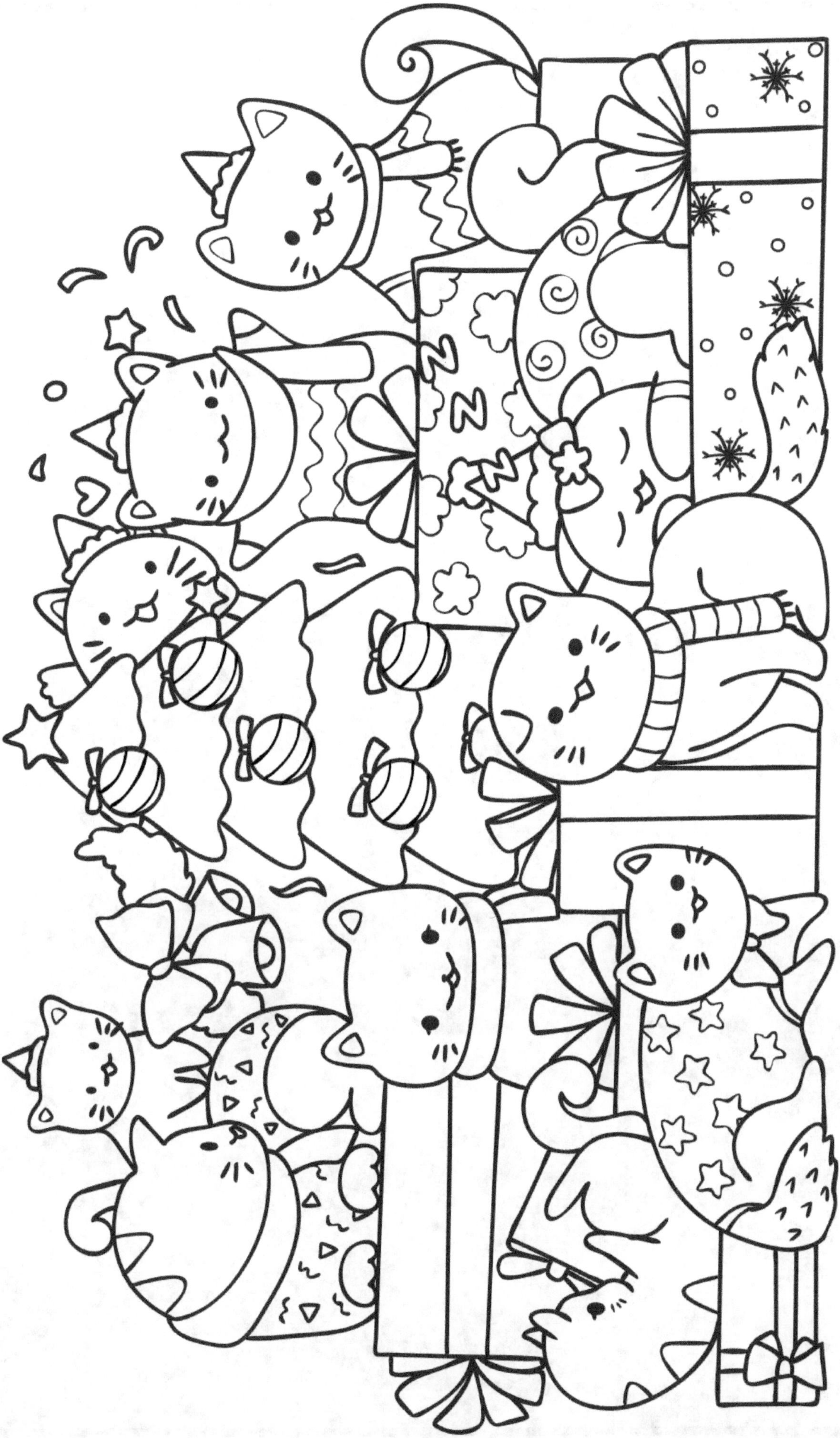
Z Z Z

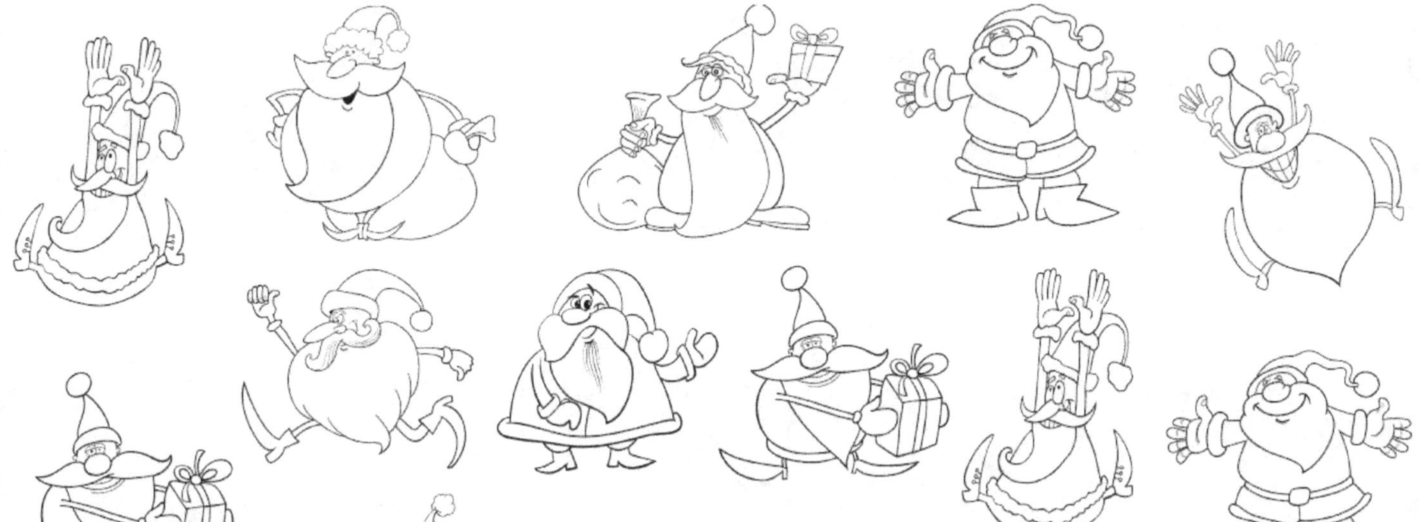
CHRISTMAS
FIND
ONE
OF A KIND
ANSWER

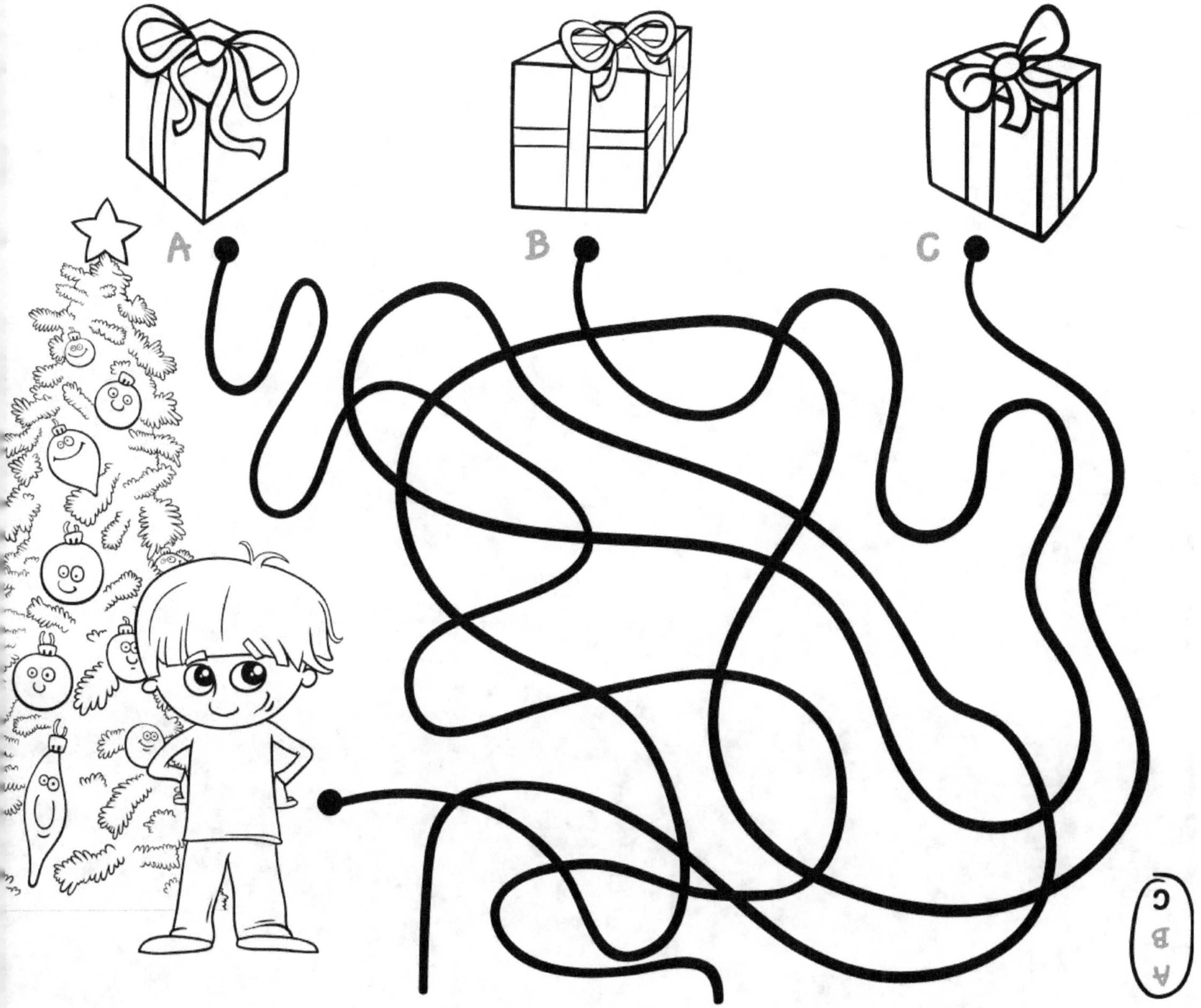
A
B
C

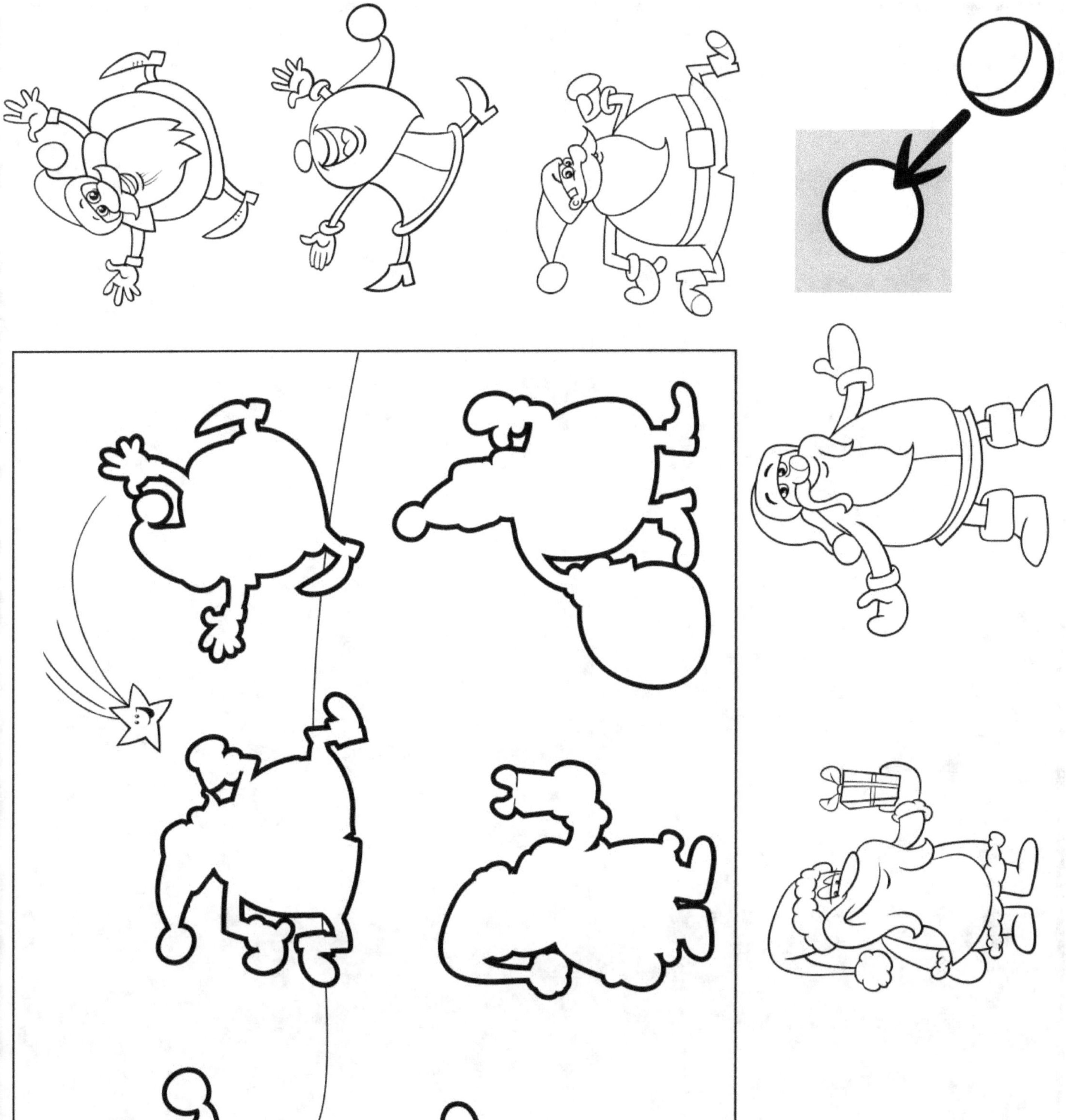

1

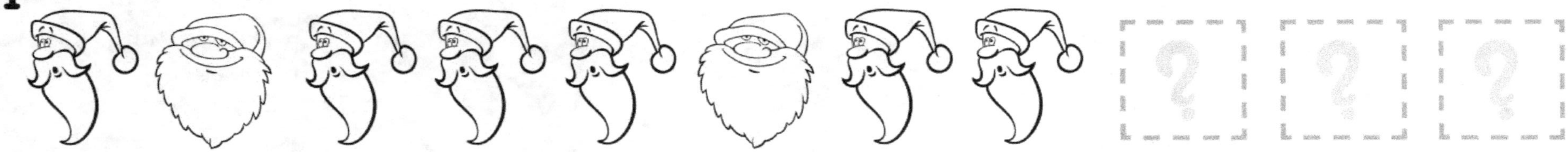

2

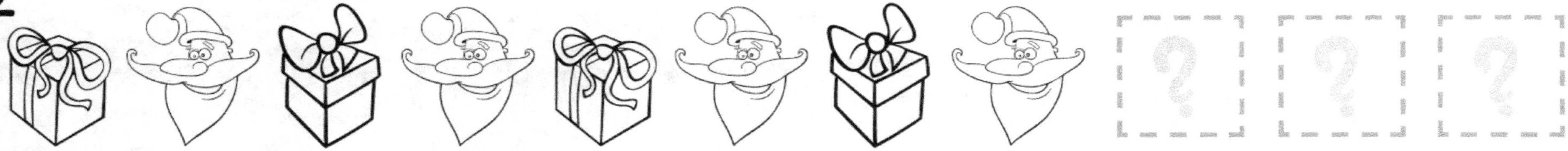

3

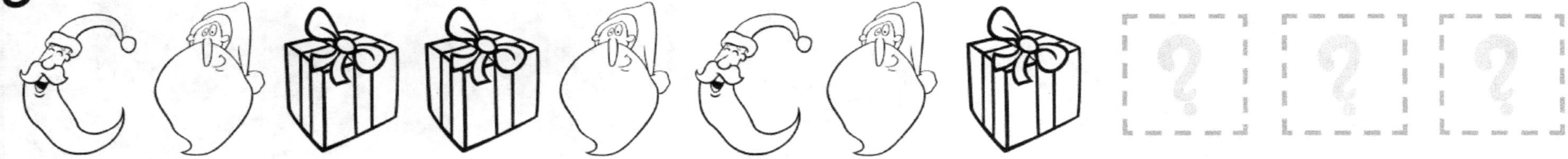

4

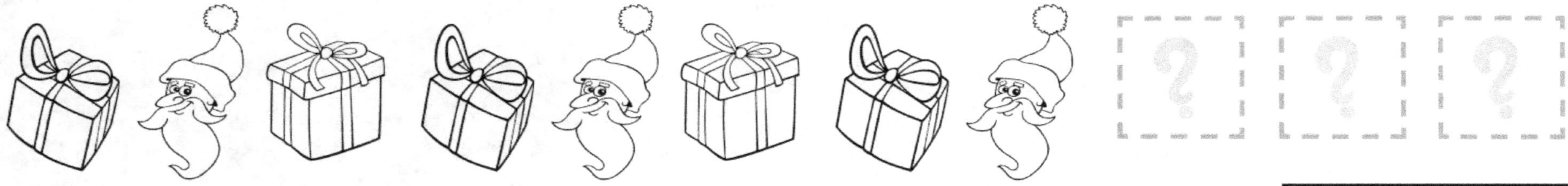

WHAT COMES NEXT?

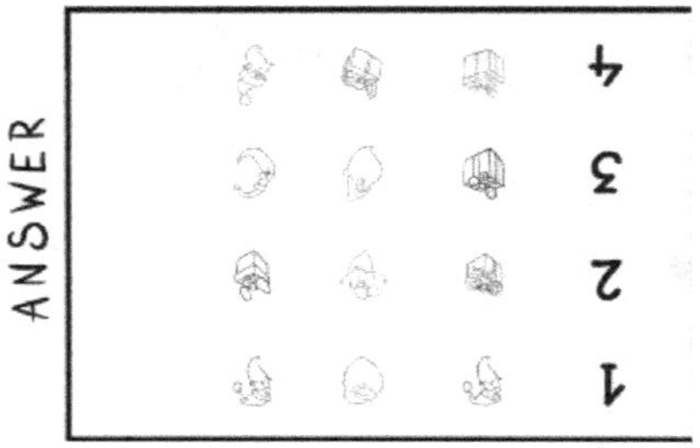

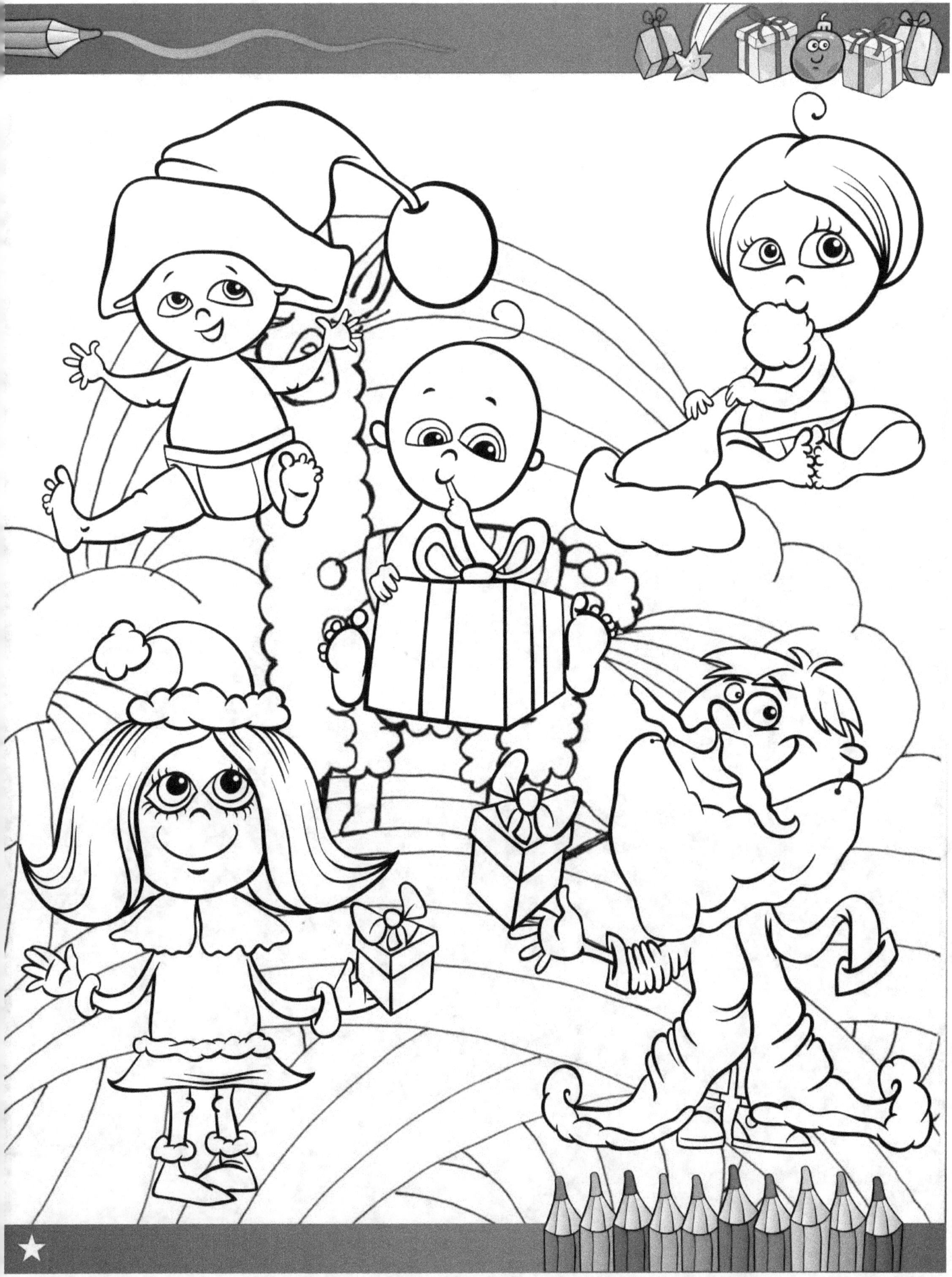

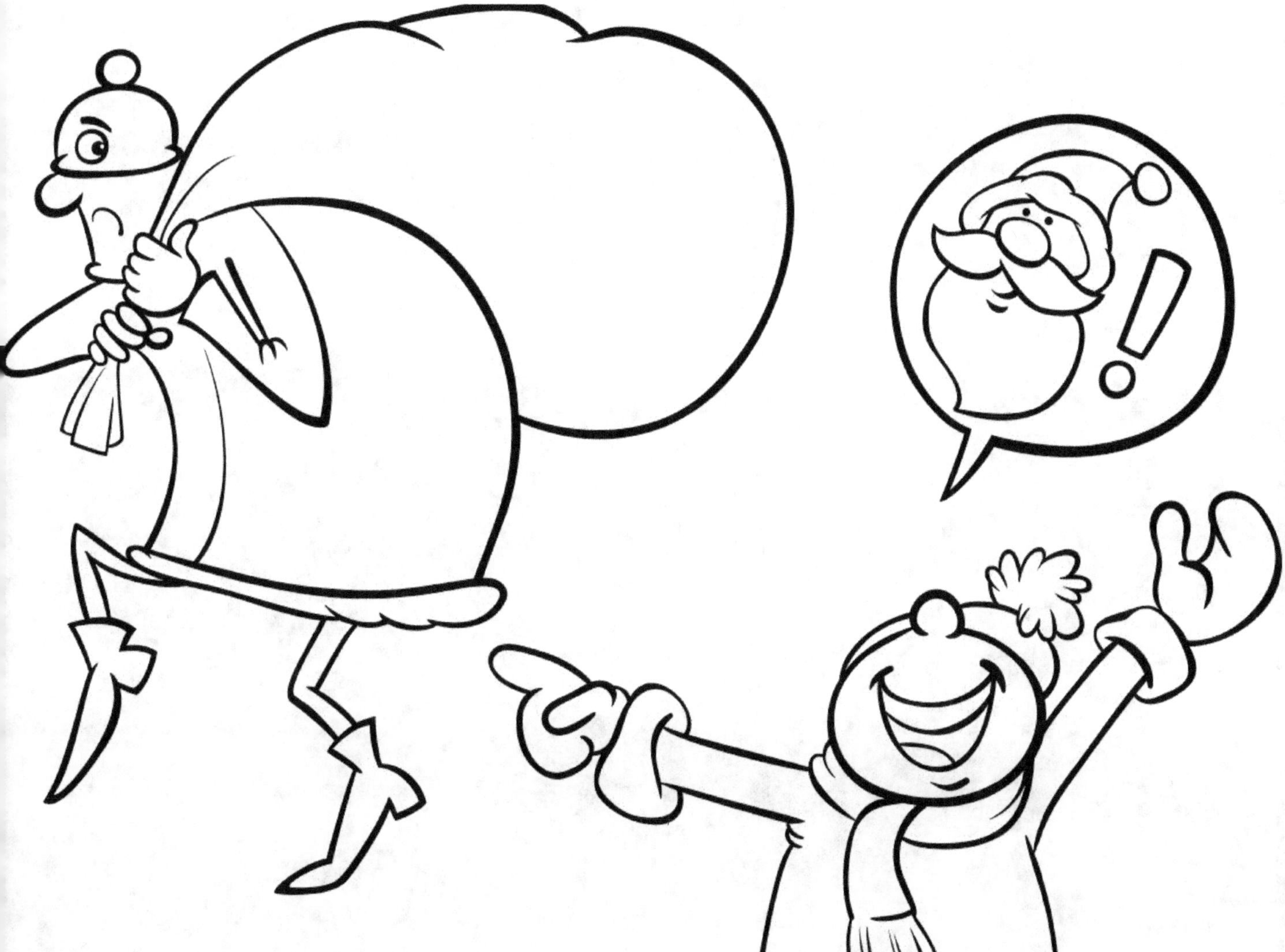

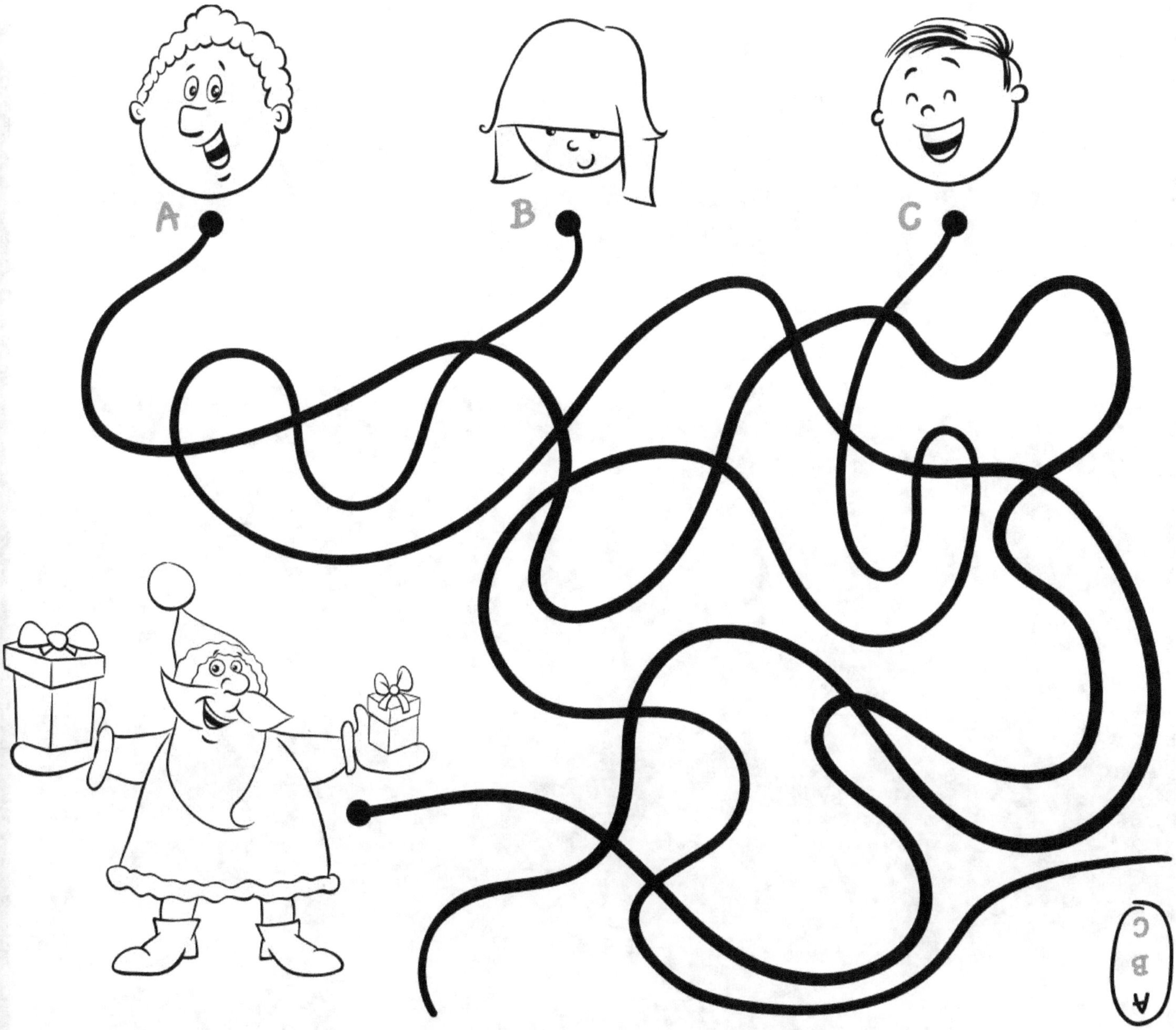
A
B
C

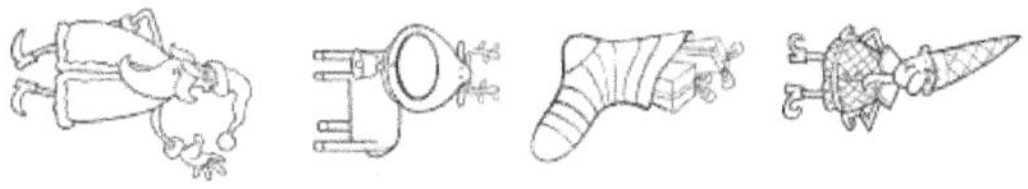

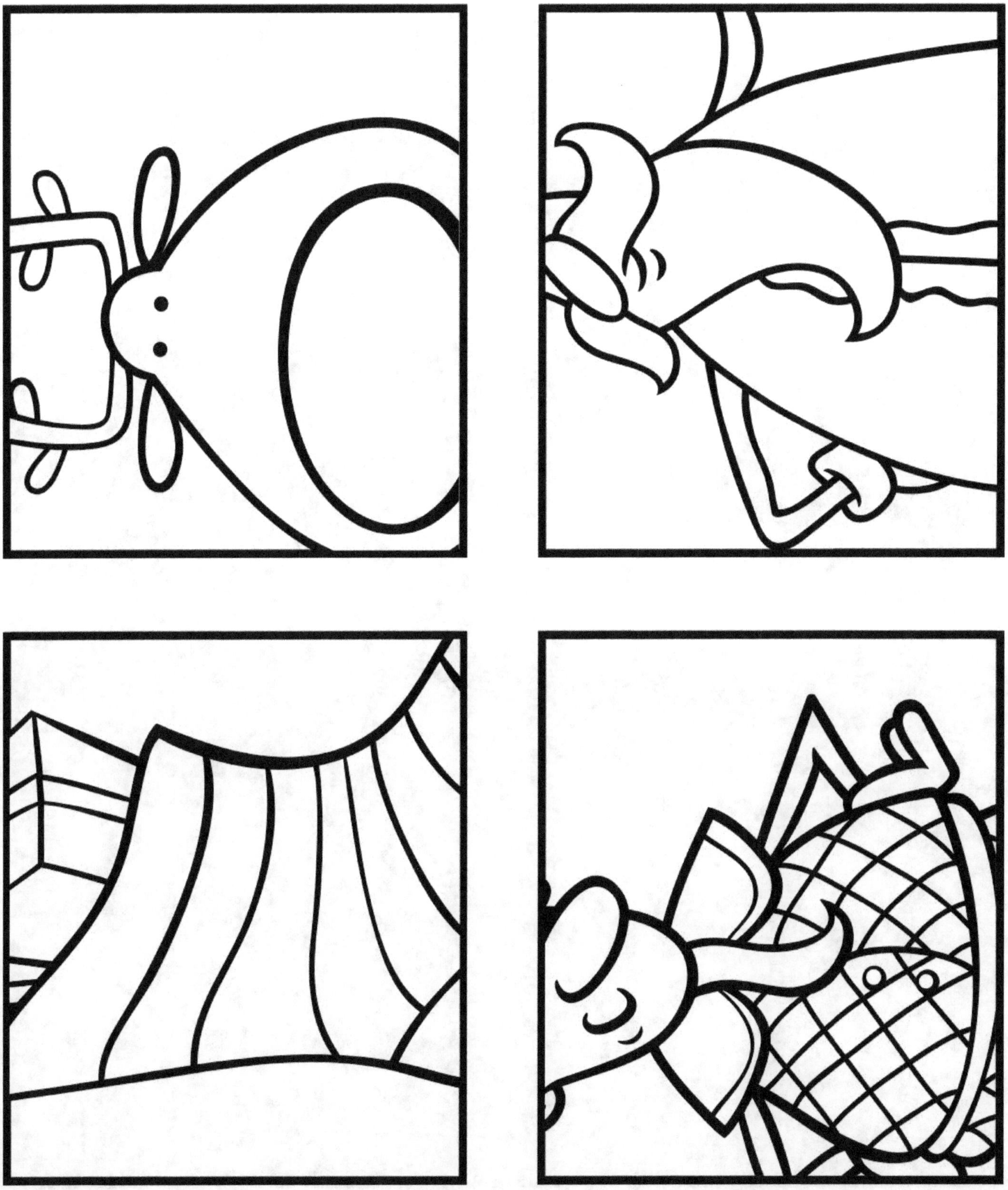

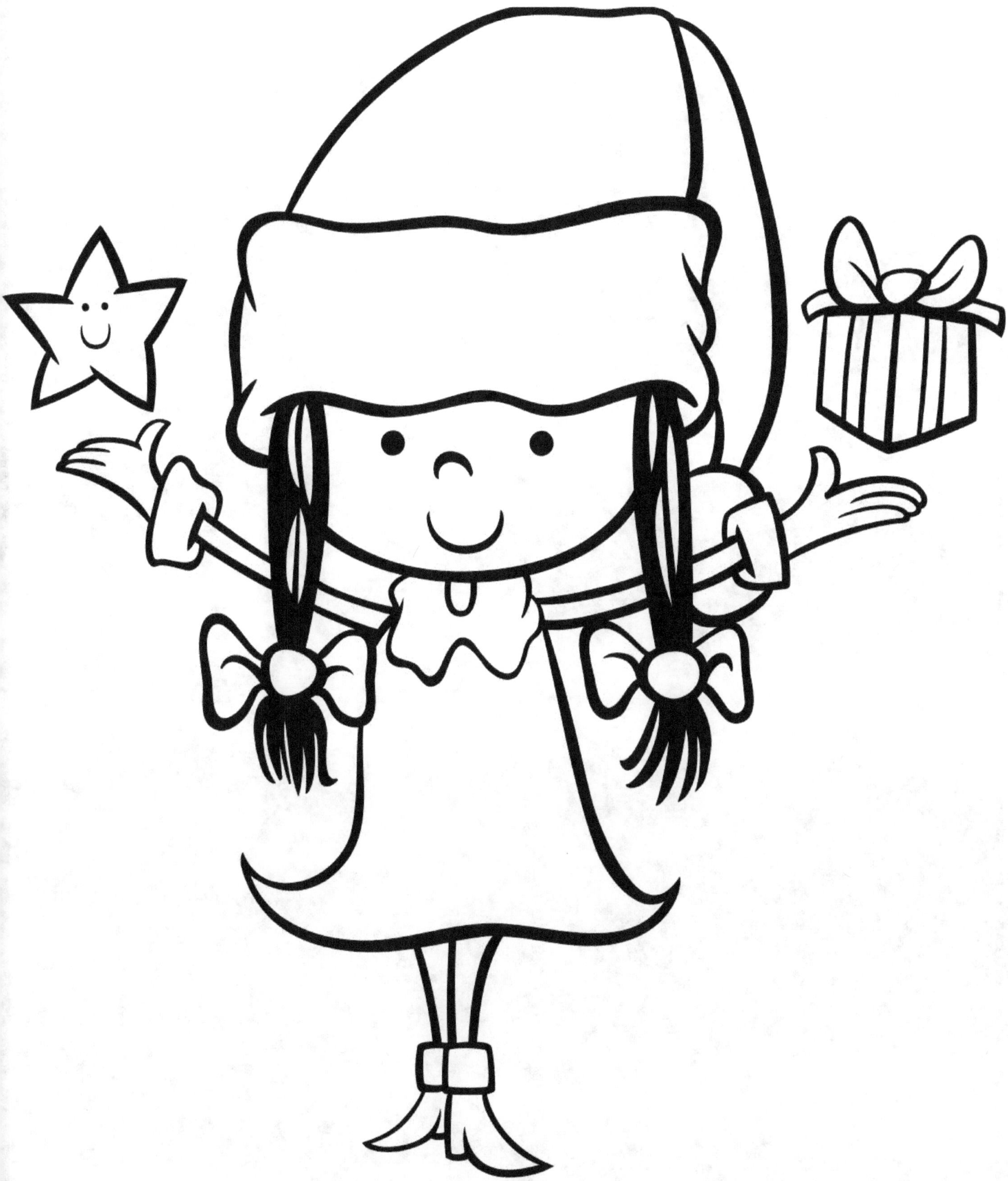

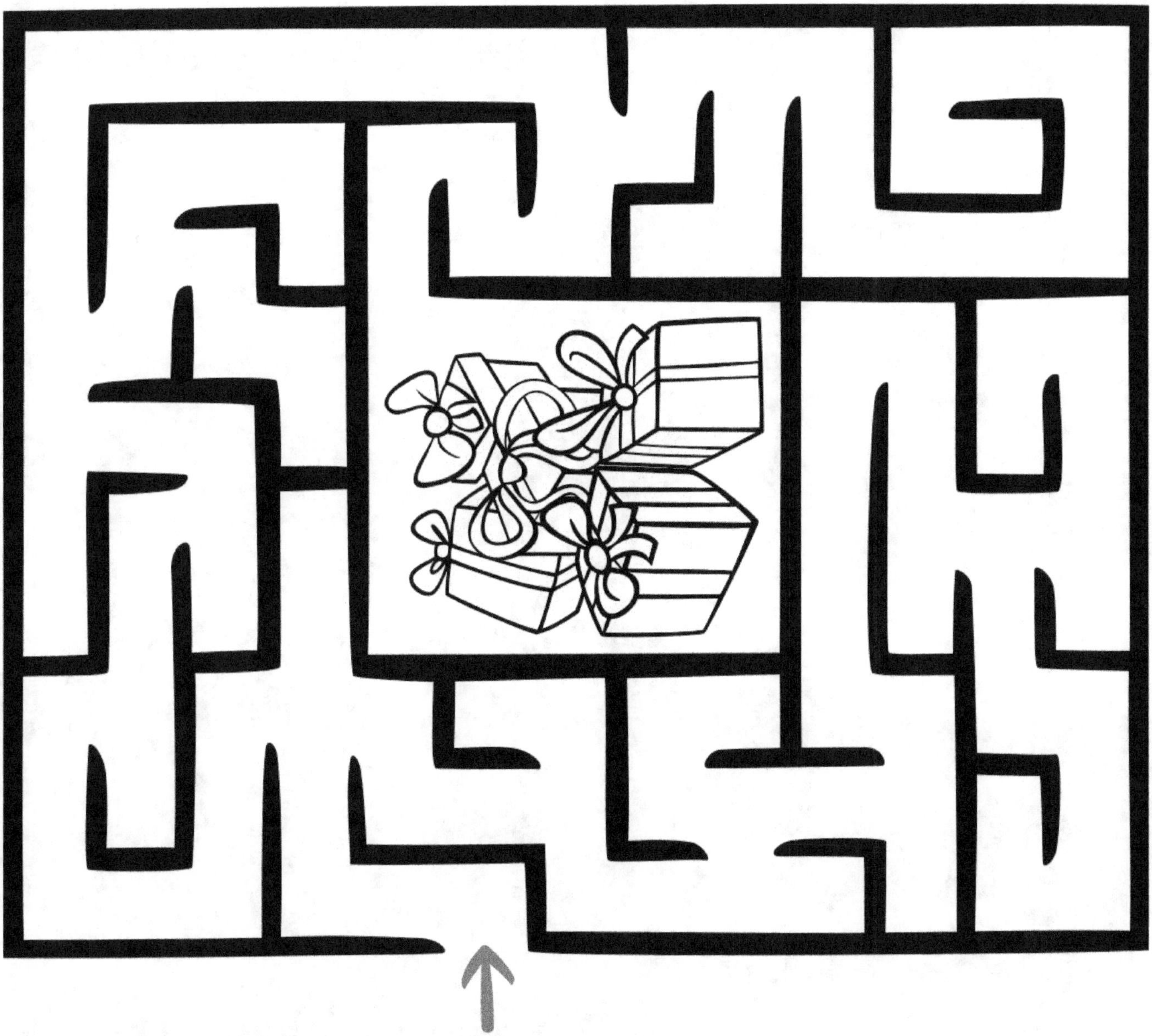

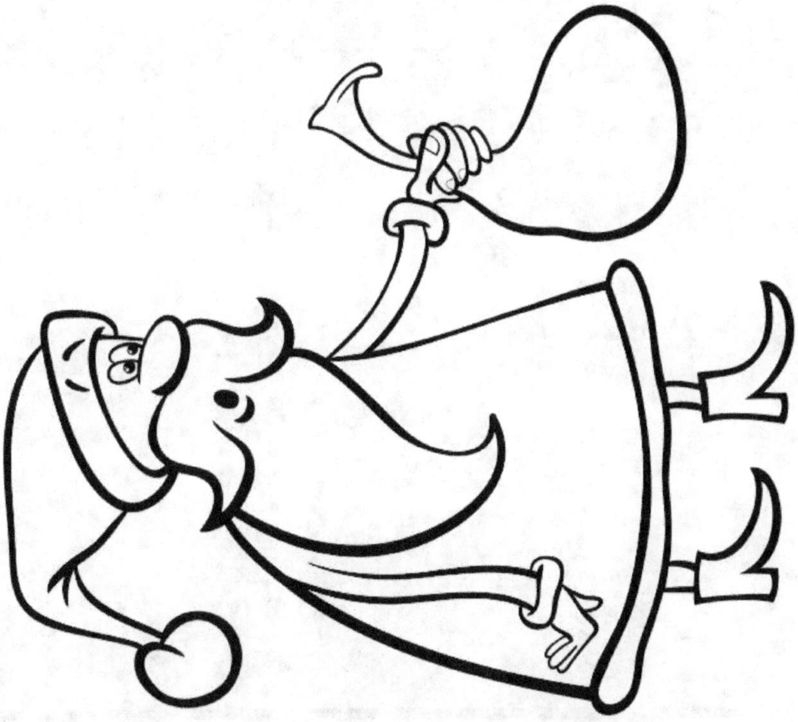

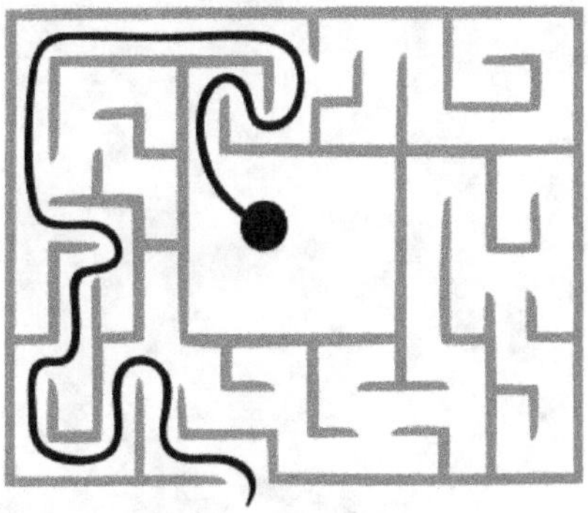

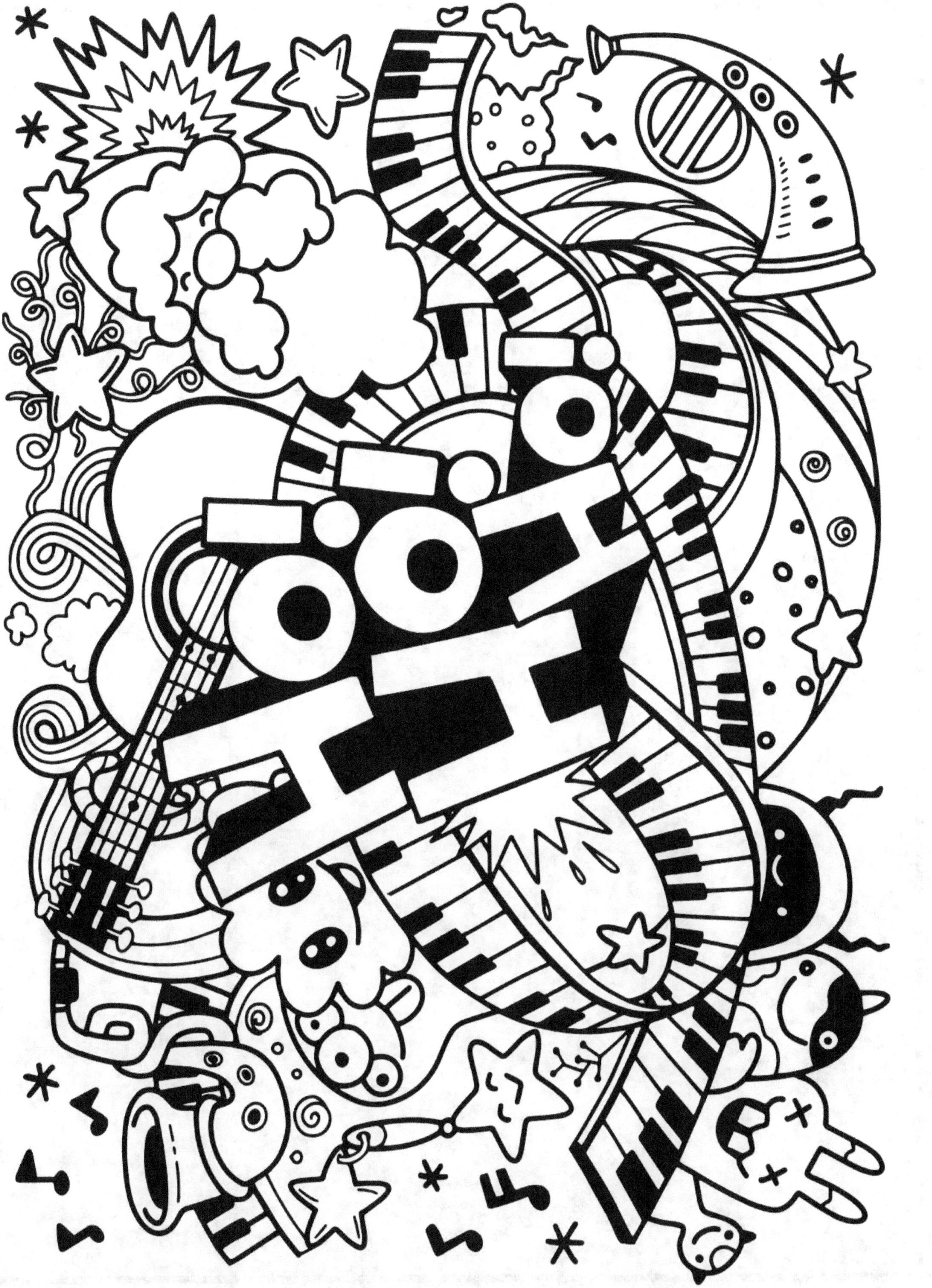

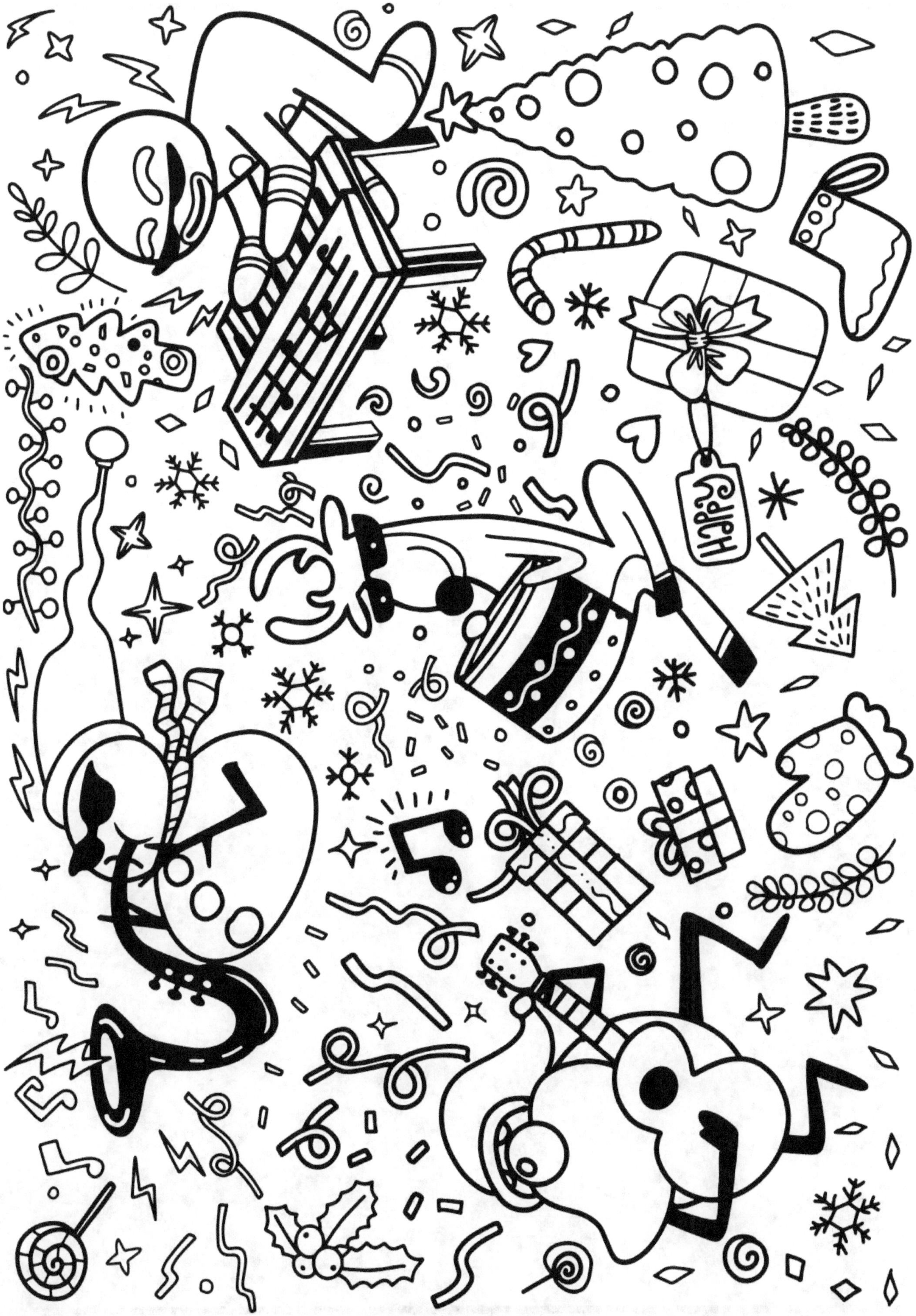

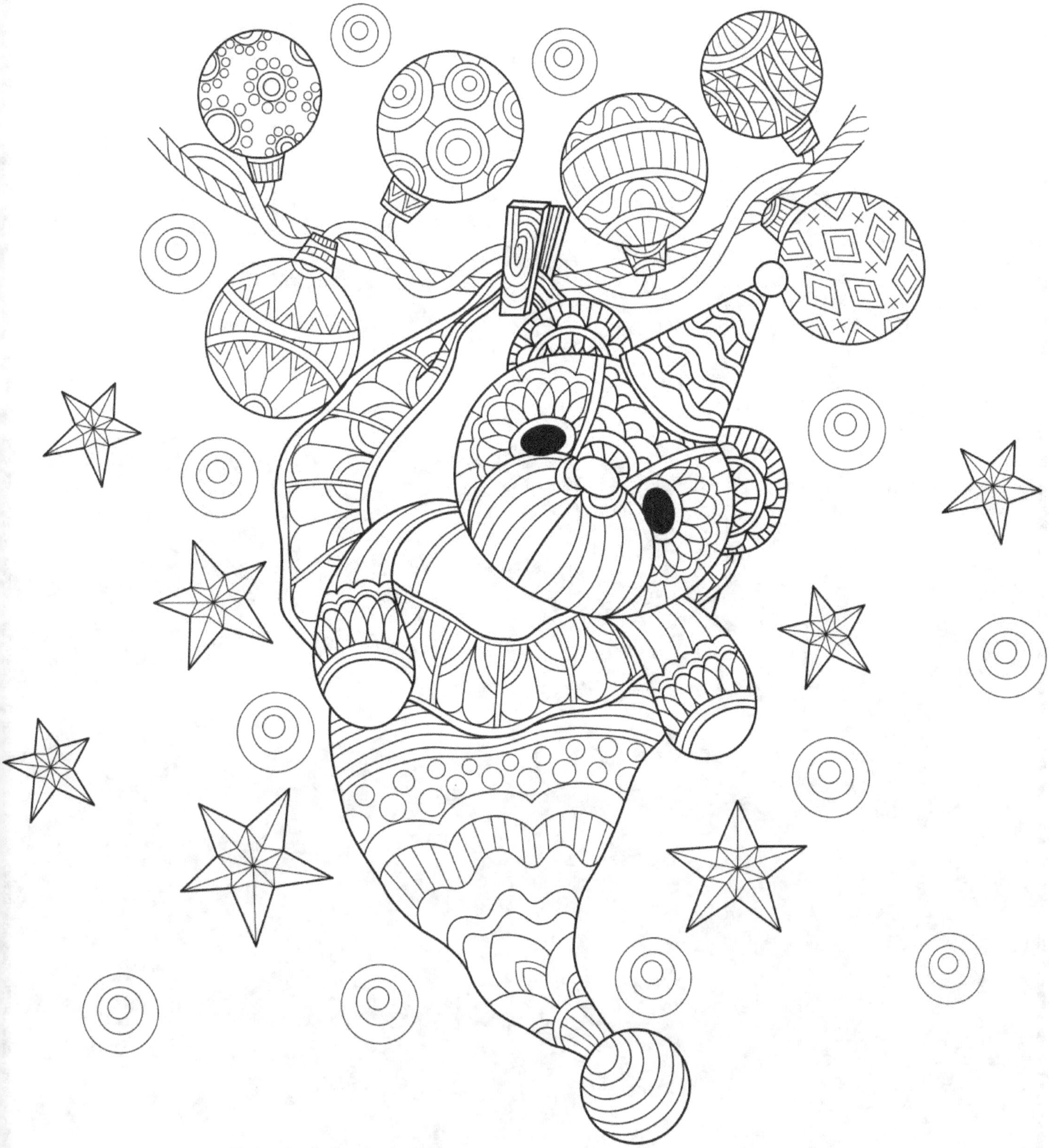

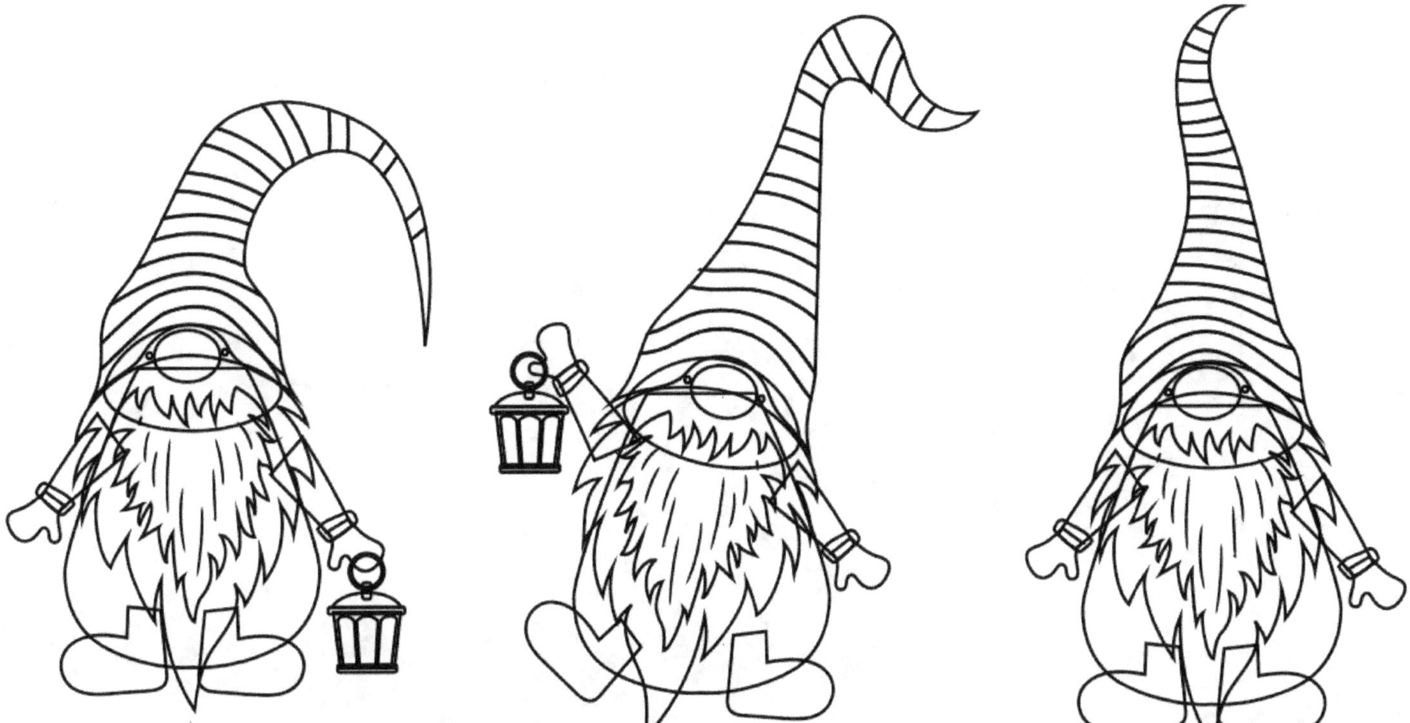

SCANDINAVIAN CHRISTMAS GNOMES

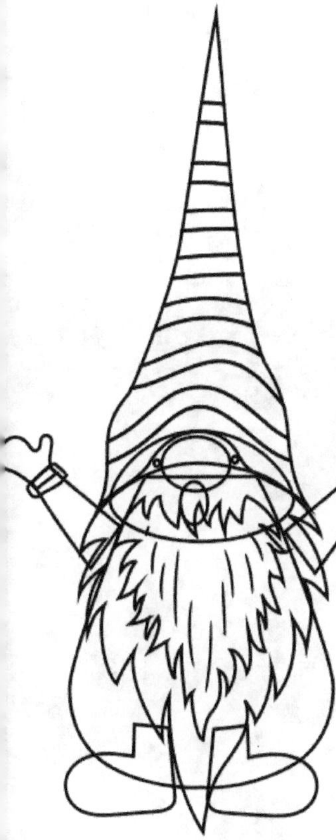

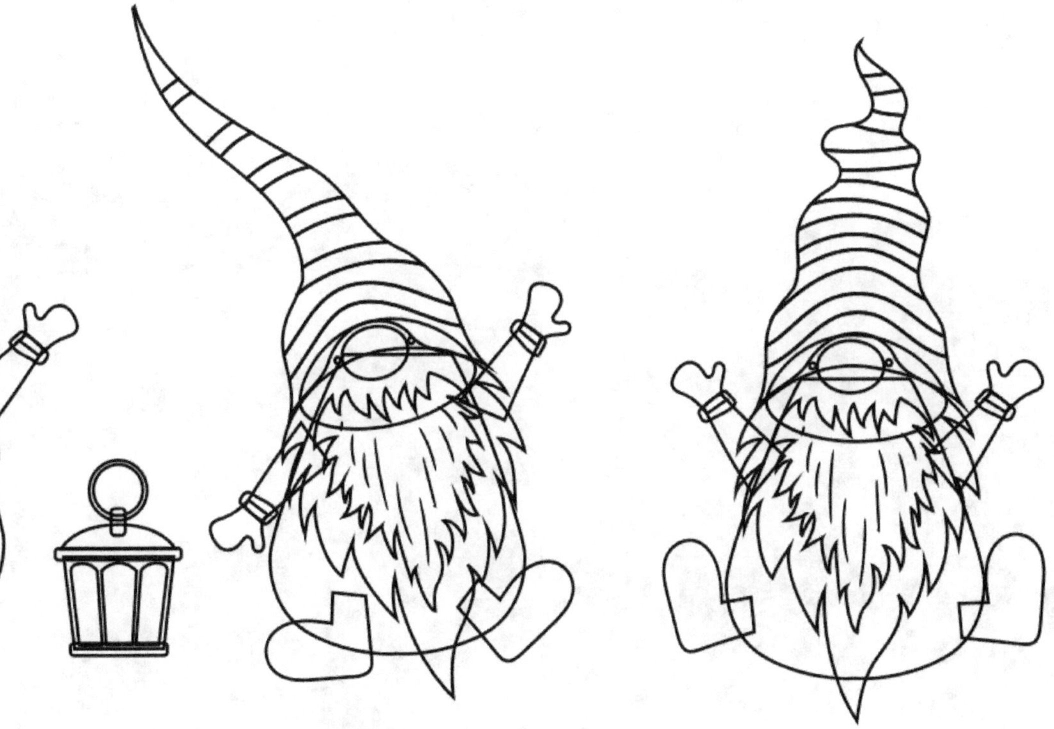

www.ingramcontent.com/pod-product-compliance
Lightning Source LLC
Chambersburg PA
CBHW081544220526
45467CB00010B/3320